# FIRST AMERICANS
# The Mohawk

## DAVID C. KING

 Marshall Cavendish
Benchmark
New York

# ACKNOWLEDGMENTS

Series consultant: Raymond Bial

Marshall Cavendish Benchmark
99 White Plains Road
Tarrytown, New York 10591
www.marshallcavendish.us

Text, maps, and illustrations copyright © 2010 by Marshall Cavendish Corporation
Map illustrations by Rodica Prato
Craft illustrations by Chris Santoro

Library of Congress Cataloging-in-Publication Data
King, David C.
The Mohawk / by David C. King.
p. cm. — (First Americans)
Includes bibliographical references and index.
Summary: "Provides comprehensive information on the background, lifestyle,
beliefs, and present-day lives of the Mohawk people"—Provided by publisher.
ISBN 978-0-7614-4132-8
1. Mohawk Indians—History—Juvenile literature. 2. Mohawk
Indians—Social life and customs—Juvenile literature. I. Title.
E99.M8K56 2010
974.7004'975542—dc22
2008042000

Front cover: A Mohawk child with a painted face and fur headdress attends an event in Cornwall, New York.
Title page: A seventeenth-century hand-colored woodcut of the totem or tribe-mark of the Five Iroquois Nations
Photo research by Connie Gardner
Cover photo by Michael S. Yamashita/Corbis

The photographs in this book are used by permission and through the courtesy of: *North Wind Picture Archive*: 1;
*Corbis*: Lee Snider/Photo Images, 4; Ted Spiegel, 26; Earl H. Nazima Kowall, 40; Richard Cooke, 33;
*The Granger Collection*: 7, 10, 28; *Bridgeman Art Library*: Torch Light Fishing in North America, John Heaviside,
8; When The Red Man Rode The Iroquo, Ron Embleton, 9; Island of Manhattan, American School, 14; *Alamy*:
Mary Evans Picture Library, 13; Philip Scalia, 17; North Wind Picture Archive, 18; *Getty Images*: Bridgeman Art
Library, 21; Hulton Archive, 30; *Native Stock*; Marilyn Angel Wynn, 24, 32.

Editor: Deborah Grahame
Publisher: Michelle Bisson
Art Director: Anahid Hamparian
Series Designer: Symon Chow

Printed in Malaysia
1 3 5 6 4 2

# CONTENTS

# 1 · THE KEEPERS OF THE EASTERN DOOR

For several centuries, the area that became New York State was occupied by the Five Nations of the Iroquois Confederacy. The Five were prosperous and strong. Their eastern territory was the land of the Mohawk. They were known as the Keepers of the Eastern Door, protecting the Confederacy from anyone advancing from the East—that is, New England.

Like the other Iroquois nations, the Mohawk lived in large wood-and-bark structures, known as **longhouses**, with as many as twenty families living in each house. The Iroquois people call themselves the **Haudenosaunee**, or the "People of the Longhouse."

Several longhouses were clustered together into villages, and each village was surrounded by a defensive **stockade**, or **palisade**, a wall of tall poles sharpened at the top. When

A modern reproduction of a bark longhouse stands at a state historic site in New York.

Dutch explorers first saw these large walled villages, they called them "castles" because they looked so strong.

Until nearly 1800, the traditional home of the Mohawk was centered on the large, fertile land of the Mohawk Valley. Today, travelers crossing New York State can still see the majestic sweep of the valley and the Mohawk River, which forms part of the Erie Canal. The traditional homeland stretched from their western boundary with the Oneida Nation as far east as present-day Vermont and north to the St. Lawrence River.

Low, gentle hills surround the valley, most of it covered with forests. The cleared land is very fertile. The Mohawk were farmers, and they planted crops of corn, beans, squash, and pumpkins in fields just outside the stockades. The entire village moved every twelve to fourteen years when the soil began to lose its fertility.

The forests provided excellent hunting for large game, including deer, bear, and moose, as well as small game, such as rabbit, woodchuck, and a variety of birds—turkey, quail, and

A Mohawk village in central New York about 1780

migratory water fowl. Fish, too, were plentiful in streams and lakes. They were caught with bows and arrows, spears, or in large nets called **weirs**.

From the early 1500s to about 1790, the Five Nations of the Iroquois enjoyed a period of unity, prosperity, and power.

Indians fished at night by the light of torches.

This era began with the formation of the Iroquois Confederacy through the Great Law of Peace.

In the 1600s, the Five Nations used their power to launch numerous raids on rival tribes to the north and west. The largest of those tribes—the Huron—had built a very profitable fur trade with the French, who had established the colony of New France in present-day Canada. The Native Americans traded beaver pelts for French manufactured goods, including iron or steel tools and weapons, colorful glass beads, and cotton cloth. Beaver fur had become wildly popular for making felt top hats for men in Europe.

To cut into this rich trade, a force of more than one thousand Iroquois warriors, including Mohawk, invaded the Huron lands in 1648. They destroyed dozens of villages, killed hundreds, and drove many to flee to the west, where they later became known as the Wyandot. Other Huron survivors settled in the vicinity of present-day Quebec.

Mohawk Indians invaded Huron lands and later fought against American colonists.

Also in the mid-1600s, the English had taken over the Dutch colony of New Netherland, centered in the Hudson River Valley and present-day New York City. The Iroquois became allies of the British. Many Mohawk were influenced by the agent of the British Crown, Colonel Guy Johnson, whose uncle, the previous agent, had built a substantial house in the Mohawk Valley where the Mohawk were always welcome. These close relations also led a number of Mohawk to become Christians and even adopt Christian names.

One of the most famous Mohawks was Joseph Brant (c. 1742–1807). He became an assistant to Colonel Johnson, fought on the side of the British in their war against France, and also began his life work of translating

Joseph Brant, or Thayendanegea, was one of the most famous Mohawk leaders.

the Bible into the Mohawk language. Brant continued to side with the British during the American Revolution. He became the war leader of a powerful Iroquois force made up of Mohawk, Onondaga, Cayuga, and Seneca. The two sides engaged in vicious fighting, with brutality on both sides, and Brant became known as "Monster Brant."

After the Americans won the War for Independence, Brant fled for protection to Canada because he had supported the British. He led several hundred followers into Canada, which was still a British colony. The British granted the Mohawk land along the Grand River in Ontario Province. Brant had long said that victory for the Americans would lead to a tidal wave of settlers moving into Iroquois lands. His prediction was right. In 1779, an American army of four thousand swept through Iroquois lands, burning crops and destroying villages. By the 1790s, New York was home to thousands of American settlers and it was one of the original thirteen states.

# The League of the Iroquois

The Iroquois Confederacy was probably formed about five hundred years ago, although historians are not certain of the date. It was also known as the League of the Iroquois. According to Mohawk oral tradition, the idea for creating a union of the Five Iroquois Nations was the inspiration of a Huron prophet named Deganwidah and his spokesman, Hiawatha, a Mohawk. Until this pair entered the scene, the Five Nations had warred against each other almost constantly. In the nineteenth century, American poet Henry Wadsworth Longfellow wrote a long poem about Hiawatha, but its historical facts are not very accurate.

Hiawatha negotiated with the Iroquois chiefs, presenting Deganwidah's ideas. For unknown reasons, Deganwidah had great difficulty speaking so Hiawatha spoke for him. The result was a plan of government—a constitution—called the Great Law of Peace. The law created a confederacy, uniting the nations against their enemies. Women played an important role in the Confederacy. They appointed the **sachems**, or chiefs, who managed the affairs of the Confederacy. If a sachem did not perform well, the women who appointed him could replace him.

The longhouse was the symbol for the Confederacy. In this symbolism, the Seneca were the Keepers of the Western Door, and the Mohawk were Keepers of the Eastern Door. Of the three middle tribes—Oneida, Onondaga, Cayuga—the Onondaga were Keepers of the Flame. Continuing the symbolism, the Five Nations called themselves the Haudenosaunee—the People of the Longhouse.

The peace created years of prosperity and strength for the Iroquois Confederacy. In 1722 the Tuscarora moved north and were accepted as the Sixth Nation. Their united strength enabled them to send raids against neighboring tribes. Also, in the 1700s they could balance two colonial powers against each other—France to the north and Britain to the east and south.

In addition, the Confederacy government became a model for the thirteen American colonies as they considered ways to form a united government when they declared independence from Great Britain.

Henry Wadsworth Longfellow wrote a well-known poem about the legend of Hiawatha.

# 2 · A WOODLAND WAY OF LIFE

A Mohawk village was built in a forest clearing near a river or stream. The woodland provided wild game, plus roots, nuts, mushrooms, and herbs, while the stream offered fish and a constant supply of fresh water. The clearing was usually quite large, with room for ten or more longhouses set in a random pattern to prevent fires from spreading.

The daily life of the Mohawk centered in and around the longhouse. Anywhere between eight and twenty families lived in each longhouse; the families were usually related as members of the same **clan**.

Longhouses varied in size. Each longhouse consisted of one long room, sometimes half the length of a football field. The width was the same as the height. There were no windows— just a low doorway at each end. A central corridor ran the

Longhouses on the island of Manhattan in the years before the Dutch arrived length of the building, with fireplaces dug into the corridor floor at intervals, and holes in the roof overhead for the smoke to escape. Families lived on both sides of the corridor, and families across from each other shared the fireplace between them. Wide sleeping platforms, or bunks, were attached to the walls. A second layer of platforms, above the first, was used for storage. The platforms were divided by woven screens that marked off one-family compartments.

Mohawk today no longer live in longhouses, although a few are kept on reservations for festivals or special ceremonies.

Food was stored in several ways. Some was hung from storage racks or from rafters. Strings of corn were hung to dry along with pieces of pumpkin and other squash. And some food was stored in pits dug into the floor of the longhouse.

Food took up a good deal of each family's time: growing or gathering it; preparing and eating it; and preserving some for future use. Farming for several basic crops provided a secure food supply. The crops known as the **Three Sisters**—corn, beans, and squash—were the most important, especially

Shelves for sleeping and for storage lined the longhouse walls.

corn, because when dried, it could be stored for months.

The men prepared the field for planting and then the women took over. The bean vines wound around the corn stalks, and the squash vines spread along the ground keeping the soil cool and moist.

A large part of the Mohawk diet came from wild foods. Men and older boys often hunted in groups so they could

The Indian "Three Sisters"—corn, squash, and beans

drive deer or other game into a crude corral made of thickets and branches. They could then kill as many as needed and cut up the meat before heading home. They often dried or smoked the meat on racks to preserve it.

Women also worked together gathering wild foods. Some foods were eaten raw, including berries and nuts. Girls worked with their mothers and learned new tasks by watching. Whether gathering food, or cooking, or preserving foods, the Mohawk were constantly planning for the future. Hunger, and even starvation, were ever-present dangers. As a result, all Native Americans, including the Mohawk, preserved as much food as possible by drying or smoking it on racks, either in the sun or over a low fire.

Meals were informal. A favorite meal was a stew or thick soup, usually based on meat and corn. The meal was prepared in the morning in an iron kettle or a clay pot hung over the fire on a tripod of sturdy poles. All sorts of foods were added to the meat, corn, and water—beans, pieces of squash, mushrooms, and root foods, as well as wild potatoes or wild onions. Family members ate when they were hungry. A sit-down meal was reserved for special occasions, such as weddings or festivals.

Other basic foods were made with cornmeal, which was made from dried corn. The dried kernels were boiled in water, sometimes with wood ashes added to loosen the hulls. When dry, the corn was pounded into meal, with a mortar made of a hollowed-out log or stump and a pestle carved from a maple. The meal was then sifted through a loosely woven basket, and could then be made into a mush or mixed into dough for breadlike cakes.

The Iroquois nations grew about fifteen varieties of corn. Some varieties were best when roasted and eaten as corn on the cob. Popcorn was also popular, popped by shaking it over the fire in a covered basket.

For sweeteners, the Mohawk, like other Woodland people, enjoyed honey and maple syrup or maple sugar. Maple syrup was made by tapping maple trees in very early spring, then boiling down the sap into syrup, or boiled further into maple sugar.

Until the Mohawk began trading with Europeans and American colonists, most Indian clothing was made of soft and comfortable deerskin wrapped between the legs then up and under a belt and then over a belt in front and back. In cold weather, men and boys added **leggings**, a kind of short, kiltlike skirt, and a shirt, all made from deerskin.

Clothing for women and girls was somewhat similar. In summer they wore only a deerskin skirt with a loose shawl around the shoulders. In cool weather, they added deerskin tunics and, in severe weather, both men and women wore robes made of furs. These were small furs—rabbit, squirrel, raccoon, and others—sewn together. Everyone wore deerskin moccasins.

Men used sharp-edged flint to shave their heads except for a narrow row from front to back. This style, which is still known as a "Mohawk," was normally worn in preparation for war. At other times, Mohawk men wore a skull cap decorated with three eagle feathers. Women either wore their hair long and loose, or they tied it at the back of the neck.

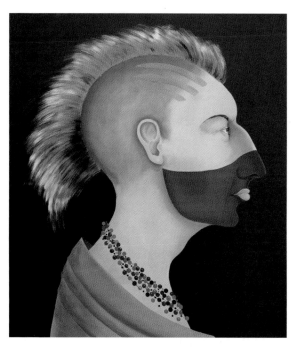

A masked warrior displays the "Mohawk" hair style.

Once there was trade with Europeans and American colonists, the Mohawk adopted their clothing styles, such as cotton blouses and shirts. Mohawk women used European beads to decorate blouses and shirts, and also to make jewelry.

Before they traded with Dutch and English colonists for metal tools, the Mohawk relied on natural materials—wood, stone, bone, shell, and horn. They were skilled at transforming these materials into durable and attractive tools and weapons, including bows and arrows, spears, hatchets, canoes, drums, and baskets.

# Bead Necklace

Native Americans in nearly all societies were skilled in making all kinds of jewelry and other forms of decorations. They used dyed porcupine quills to decorate clothing and other items. Necklaces were made of bits of bone, antler, seashell, and semiprecious stones. They drilled holes with a stone-tipped drill.

The Europeans and colonists brought colorful glass beads that the Indian peoples could not get enough of. They used the smallest beads, called seed beads, for sewing decorations on clothing, headdresses, and other items. Larger beads were used to make necklaces and other jewelry items.

Here is a project for making your own version of a Mohawk necklace. Look for two or more varieties of macaroni with holes—the more different shapes, the better.

## You will need:

- 1 or 2 sheets of newspaper
- 3 small plastic bowls or paper cups
- teaspoon
- ¼ cup (60 milliliters) rubbing alcohol
- red, blue, yellow food coloring
- 15–20 pieces of elbow macaroni
- paper towels
- 18–20 inches (45–50 centimeters) of string

**1.** Spread the newspaper over your work surface.

**2.** Pour 5 or 6 teaspoons (25 or 30 ml) of rubbing alcohol into each of the 3 cups or bowls.

**3.** Add enough red, blue, and yellow food coloring to make a rich color.

**4.** Place $^1/_3$ of the macaroni in each bowl. Stir the pieces with the teaspoon in 1 bowl for about 10 seconds, rinse the spoon, and repeat with the other 2 bowls.

**5.** Pour off the colored alcohol and place the colored "beads" on paper towels to dry. Drying time will vary.

**6.** String the beads in whatever pattern looks pleasing and tie the ends in a double knot. Your Mohawk necklace is ready to wear.

Mohawk men displayed their skills in making many items, and none is admired more than their skill in making elm-bark canoes. Several men worked together to make the frame out of elm or white birch. With a stone hammer and

The Woodland and Algonquian tribes were famed for their skill in crafting canoes.

wedges, they split the framing wood into thin boards. Boards and poles were then formed into the frame. They placed the frame between sheets of bark on the ground, then pulled up the bark on either side of the frame and laced it to the frame with pieces of long, thin root fibers. The bow and stern were bent into a point so that it could move through the water with speed and ease of steering. The bow and stern were also raised a little for protection in rough water.

The thin cedar or birch boards made up the inside bottom of the canoe and every seam was sealed with heated pine resin. Europeans and American colonists were amazed by the beauty, speed, and durability of the canoes.

# 3 · MOHAWK CUSTOMS AND BELIEFS

The Mohawk lived in large, **extended families** that included aunts and uncles, grandparents, and cousins. Children traced heritage through their mother's family.

Each family usually had just two or three children. The children were treated with great love. They were surrounded by family members but they also learned to be independent and courageous. Every day was a learning day for boys and girls of all ages. Their teachers were every older family member, especially of course the parents. The children also learned that it was important to make their families proud of them. Being considerate and helpful to adults was one way of achieving that goal. It was also important not to complain about such things as pain, or being hungry, or hot or cold.

Girls learned adult skills by watching their mothers and working with them. They also observed the ways in which

A Mohawk man and boy participate in a tribal event in Ontario, Canada.

Women played an important part in making decisions for the Mohawk and other Iroquois nations.

village women worked together. They learned to gather wild foods, tend to crops, help prepare meals, and to store foods. They also learned to make clothing, to construct baskets, make clay pots, and engage in all the tasks their mothers engaged in.

In similar ways, boys learned by following their fathers and older brothers. By age nine or ten, they could go along on hunting and fishing trips, following family members closely. By age twelve or thirteen they were sent on a solo hunting trip to track and bring in the first game. They also worked with adults on such tasks as making bows, arrows, snow shoes, and canoes.

At about age thirteen, a boy went alone, without food, into the forest on what is called a **vision quest**. He fasted to induce dreams to discover what he would later become in life. A guardian spirit, often an animal or bird, would appear and foretell the boy's future. The boy identified with this guardian spirit for the rest of his life.

Festivals, anniversaries, and other celebrations provided villagers with plenty of opportunities to have fun. They also enjoyed a variety of games, some with two people, some with two teams. Like other Indians, the Mohawk played simple games of chance, such as hiding a peach pit in one of three toy moccasins, while the opponent tried to guess the location. A certain number of correct guesses was a win.

Some games were important for sharpening skills, or building strength and coordination. One game of this type involved throwing a spear through a rolling hoop. Lacrosse, a game created by the Iroquois, was extremely rough, whether played by two teams of a few players or with teams of thirty or more. Races, wrestling, bow-and-arrow shooting contests,

Mohawk and other tribes were especially fond of lacrosse, a game invented by Native Americans.

along with winter sports, such as toboggan races or snowsnake (a game of sliding a narrow pole, or snowsnake, down a track of packed snow) were just a few of the other contests that the Mohawk enjoyed throughout the year.

Like other Indian nations, the Mohawk believed that everything had a spirit or soul. That included inanimate objects, such as stones, clouds, and rivers, as well as every living creature. Throughout the year, many festivals and celebrations offered thanks to various gods.

A Mohawk prayer, shared by other Iroquois nations, included these statements of thanksgiving:

*"We give thanks to our Mother, the Earth, which sustains us.*
*"We give thanks to the rivers and streams which supply us with water.*
*"We give thanks to all the herbs which furnish us with medicine to cure our diseases.*
*"We give thanks to the corn, and to her sisters, the beans and squashes, which give us life. . . ."*

Adapted from a display at the Schoharie Museum
of the Iroquois Indians, Schoharie, New York

When a Mohawk was ill, family members were likely to call on the False Face Society for help. They came in a group, each healer wearing a grotesque wooden mask. Crouching low to the ground, they emitted strange sounds and shook turtle-shell rattles. They then sprinkled ashes and herbs, and said

A false face mask

prayers to drive out the evil spirit.

The Mohawk—and other Iroquois—believed that illness was caused by evil spirits. These spirits were heads without bodies. They lived in the forest and spread illness from village to village. The members of the healing society carved masks into a living tree. When a carving was finished and painted, the healer cut it from the tree. The mask was designed to confuse and frighten the spirit, causing it to flee.

# "The Lily of the Mohawk"

Her Indian name was Kateri Tekakwitha (1656–1680). When she was four, she was the only member of her family to survive a smallpox epidemic, although it also affected her health, too. She was influenced by three Jesuits; they were the first Christians she had ever met.

She listened to the three men and, when she was twenty, she was instructed in the religion and was baptized with the Christian name Katherine. People in her village hated her decision. After she was stoned and threatened with torture or death, she fled 200 miles (322 kilometers) to a Christian Indian mission near Montreal.

Katherine came to be known as "The Lily of the Mohawk" for her kindness, her faith, her good life, and for the suffering she had endured. Accounts of her life, written by missionaries, provided the documentation for her canonization (the process of becoming a saint) which began in 1884. She was **beatified** by Pope John Paul II in 1980. The National Shrine of Blessed Kateri Tekakwitha is located in Fonda, New York.

PROVINCE OF QUÉBEC

KANEHSATAKE

KAHNAWAKE

MONTREAL

WAHTA

LAKE HURON

CANADA

TYENDINAGA

ST. LAWRENCE RIVER

AKWESASNE
GANIENKEH

VERMONT

MOHAWK

KANATSIOHAREKE

LAKE ONTARIO

ONEIDA

MOHAWK RIVER

MOHAWK VALLEY

SENECA

CAYUGA

ONONDAGA

TUCSCARORA

LAKE ERIE

NEW YORK

HUDSON RIVER

CAYUGA LAKE

PENNSYLVANIA

MOHAWK

# 4 · THE MODERN MOHAWK

The Iroquois Confederacy became deeply divided during the American Revolution (1775–1783), with most Mohawk siding with the British. They feared that an American victory would lead to a flood of settlers. That is precisely what happened.

By 1791 New York State took over most Mohawk lands. Only 6 square miles (15.5 square kilometers) remained in Mohawk hands. For the next 150 years, the Mohawk struggled to survive. Their communities were scattered through **reservations** in eastern New York and **reserves** in southern Ontario Province.

Many Mohawk suffered through years of poverty. In Canada, the government hoped to force or persuade them to melt into the majority population. Children were sent to English-speaking boarding schools. Separated from their families, they began to lose contact with their culture and the Mohawk language.

Some people managed to earn an income through farming,

This map shows the traditional homelands of the Five Nations of the Iroquois Confederacy.

Boarding schools tended to isolate young Mohawk from their own culture and traditions.

and Mohawk women's baskets were popular and sold well. Beginning in the 1880s, Mohawk men who dared to risk their lives built bridges, and, later, working far above the street, helped to build skyscrapers. While men from other tribes worked the "**high steel**," it was the Mohawk men who became famous for this courageous occupation. The money they brought back to their reservations helped to boost the local economy.

Throughout the twentieth century, the American people

and the government periodically recognized the plight of the reservation Indians throughout the United States and Canada, and occasionally steps were taken to improve conditions. The Mohawk themselves pressed for greater improvement. In the 1950s they began blocking roads and bridges in protest of government inaction.

Since 1970 the Mohawk have filed a number of lawsuits for return of land that they claim was taken in violation of a 1790 treaty. Some land has been restored to the tribe. In 1977, for example, the Mohawk community of Granienkeh was built on restored land. Also, a Mohawk casino was approved by New York State in 2007 and is now operational.

In addition, the Mohawk have been leaders in restoring their traditional language and culture. In 1979, parents on the Akwesasne Reservation (which straddles the St. Lawrence River) started the Akwesasne Freedom School. The school offers courses in Mohawk language and culture, as well as math, reading, history, and science. The reservation also publishes several newspapers to inform people about Mohawk life.

# Walking the High Steel

In 1886 several Mohawk men were hired to work as laborers on a bridge from Canada over the St. Lawrence River to Mohawk land in New York State. Their employers were amazed by their courage and skill in "walking the high steel" of the bridge frame.

That started a practice that has continued into the twenty-first century. The Mohawk call it **booming out** from their reservations in search of their next job of working on another high-steel structure. In the 1920s Mohawk gained even greater fame by working on the towering structures that were to make up New York City's skyline: the Empire State Building, the Chrysler Building, and the George Washington Bridge. In the 1930s one group spent time in California working on the Golden Gate Bridge.

After World War II (1939–1945) many Mohawk ironworkers moved to New York City. As many as seven hundred families moved to Brooklyn. In the 1960s many worked on the World Trade Center, proud to be working on the world's tallest buildings. After the terrorist attack of September 11, 2001, younger Mohawk went to the site to clean up debris from the buildings their parents and grandparents had helped to erect.

A Mohawk ironworker named Kyle Karonhiaktatie Beauvais explained how they work:

*A lot of people think Mohawks aren't afraid of heights; that's not true. We have as much fear as the next guy. But we deal with it differently. We also have the experience of the old timers to follow and the responsibility to lead the younger guys. There's pride in 'walking the high steel.'*

The Smithsonian Institution sponsored a traveling exhibition called "Booming Out: Mohawk Ironworkers Build New York," which toured the country from 2004 through 2007.

Mohawk ironworkers

Other outreach programs include **powwows** to which the general public is invited. A powwow gives people a chance to sample many aspects of Indian culture, including food, dance, music, and crafts.

Mohawk drummers play at a radio station in Montreal, Canada.

# Mohawk Communities Today

The Mohawk now live in eight different settlements scattered throughout eastern New York and southeastern Canada:

- Two settlements in northeastern New York: *Ganienkeh* and *Kanatsiohareke*;

- *Akwesasne* (also known as St. Regis) straddles the border between New York and Ontario;

- *Kanesatake* and *Kahnawake* in southern Quebec;

- *Tyendinaga* and *Wahta* in southern Ontario;

- Mohawk also form a majority of mixed Iroquois reserve called Six Nations of the Grand River in Ontario.

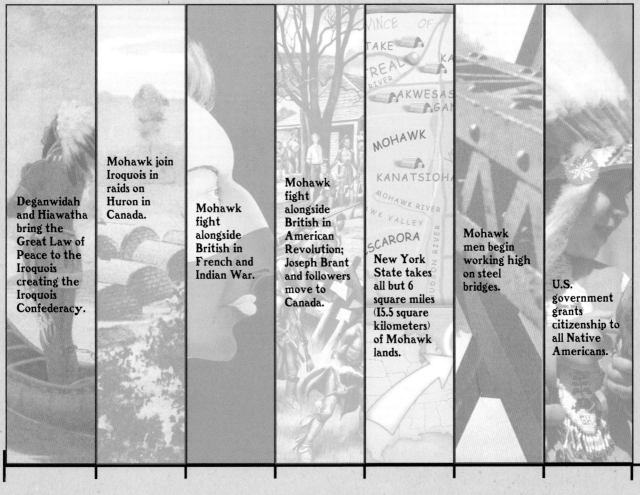

Deganwidah and Hiawatha bring the Great Law of Peace to the Iroquois creating the Iroquois Confederacy.

Mohawk join Iroquois in raids on Huron in Canada.

Mohawk fight alongside British in French and Indian War.

Mohawk fight alongside British in American Revolution; Joseph Brant and followers move to Canada.

New York State takes all but 6 square miles (15.5 square kilometers) of Mohawk lands.

Mohawk men begin working high on steel bridges.

U.S. government grants citizenship to all Native Americans.

| Early 1500s | 1648–1650 | 1756–1763 | 1775–1783 | 1790 | 1886 | 1924 |

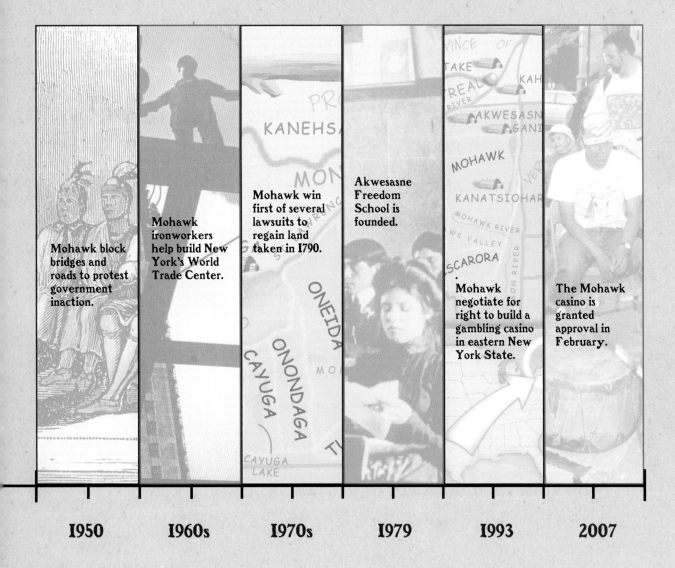

Mohawk block bridges and roads to protest government inaction.

Mohawk ironworkers help build New York's World Trade Center.

Mohawk win first of several lawsuits to regain land taken in 1790.

Akwesasne Freedom School is founded.

Mohawk negotiate for right to build a gambling casino in eastern New York State.

The Mohawk casino is granted approval in February.

1950　　1960s　　1970s　　1979　　1993　　2007

# · GLOSSARY

**beatified:** Declared to be a person who has entered heaven and is due honor, according to the Roman Catholic Church.

**booming out:** Mohawk term for leaving home community to find work in high steel.

**clan:** A group of related families.

**extended families:** Includes parents, brothers and sisters, grandparents, aunts, uncles, cousins.

**Haudenosaunee:** Iroquois name for themselves, meaning "People of the Longhouse."

**high steel:** Mohawk reference to working on high iron or steel frames of bridges or skyscrapers.

**leggings:** A tube-like garment worn by Iroquois men and boys.

**longhouses:** Standard Iroquois dwellings for several families, made of bark siding over a frame of poles.

**palisade:** A high wall made of upright poles built around a village for protection.

**powwows:** Gatherings of any tribe or nation, offering a sampling of crafts, costumes, food, music, and dance.

**reserves:** Canadian term for land set aside for Indians to live.

**reservations:** U.S. term for land set aside for Indians to live.

**sachems:** Leaders or chiefs; among the Iroquois, sachems were selected by women.

**stockade:** A high wall made of upright poles built around a village for protection; same as a palisade.

**Three Sisters:** The Indian term for their basic crops: corn, beans, and squash.

**vision quest:** A coming-of-age test of a youth's readiness for adulthood in which he spends time in isolation, hoping for a dream-like vision of a spirit bird or animal.

**weirs:** Large nets stretched across a stream to catch fish.

## • FIND OUT MORE

## Books

De Capua, Sarah. *First Americans: The Iroquois*. New York: Benchmark Books/Marshall Cavendish, 2006.

King, David C. *Projects About the Woodland Indians*. New York: Benchmark Books/Marshall Cavendish, 2006.

——*First People: An Illustrated History of North American Indians*. New York: DK Publishing Co., 2009.

Murdoch, David. *Eyewitness North American Indian*. New York: DK Publishing, 2005.

## Websites

www.accessgenealogy.com/native/tribes/mohawkhist.htm
www.geo.msu.edu/geo333/Mohawk.html
www.geocities.com/bigorrin/mohawk.htm

## About the Author

David C. King is an award-winning author who has written more than seventy books for children and young adults, including *The Haida*, *The Huron*, *The Inuit*, *The Navajo*, *The Nez Perce*, *The Powhatan*, *The Seminole*, and *The Sioux* in the First Americans series. He and his wife, Sharon, live in the Berkshires at the junction of New York, Massachusetts, and Connecticut. Their travels have taken them through most of the United States.

# · INDEX

Page numbers in **boldface** are illustrations.